ANTONIO
VIVALDI

THREE FLUTE CONCERTOS

PLAYBACK+
Speed • Pitch • Balance • Loop

To access audio visit:
www.halleonard.com/mylibrary

Enter Code
4072-2296-2376-6345

ISBN 978-1-59615-291-5

EXCLUSIVELY DISTRIBUTED BY
HAL•LEONARD®

Visit Hal Leonard Online at
www.halleonard.com

Contact us:
Hal Leonard
7777 West Bluemound Road
Milwaukee, WI 53213
Email: info@halleonard.com

In Europe, contact:
Hal Leonard Europe Limited
42 Wigmore Street
Marylebone, London, W1U 2RN
Email: info@halleonardeurope.com

In Australia, contact:
Hal Leonard Australia Pty. Ltd.
4 Lentara Court
Cheltenham, Victoria, 3192 Australia
Email: info@halleonard.com.au

CONTENTS

Flute Concerto in A Minor, RV440

Flute Concerto in G Major, Op. 10, No. 4

Flute Concerto in D Major, RV429

Vivaldi - Concerto in A minor, RV440

I

4

II

III

Vivaldi - Concerto in G, Op 10 No 4

II

Taps: ♩ ♩ ♩ ♩ | ♩ ♩ ♩ 𝄾 |

Largo

Vln I

III

Taps: ♩ ♩ ♩ ♩ | ♩ ♩ ♩ 𝄾 |

Allegro

Tutti

Solo

14

Vivaldi - Concerto in D, RV429

I

Taps: ♪♪♪ | ♪♪ ४ |

II

Trio
Andante   *Repeats not taken*

18

III

Taps: ♩. | ♩. | ♫♫ | ♩. |

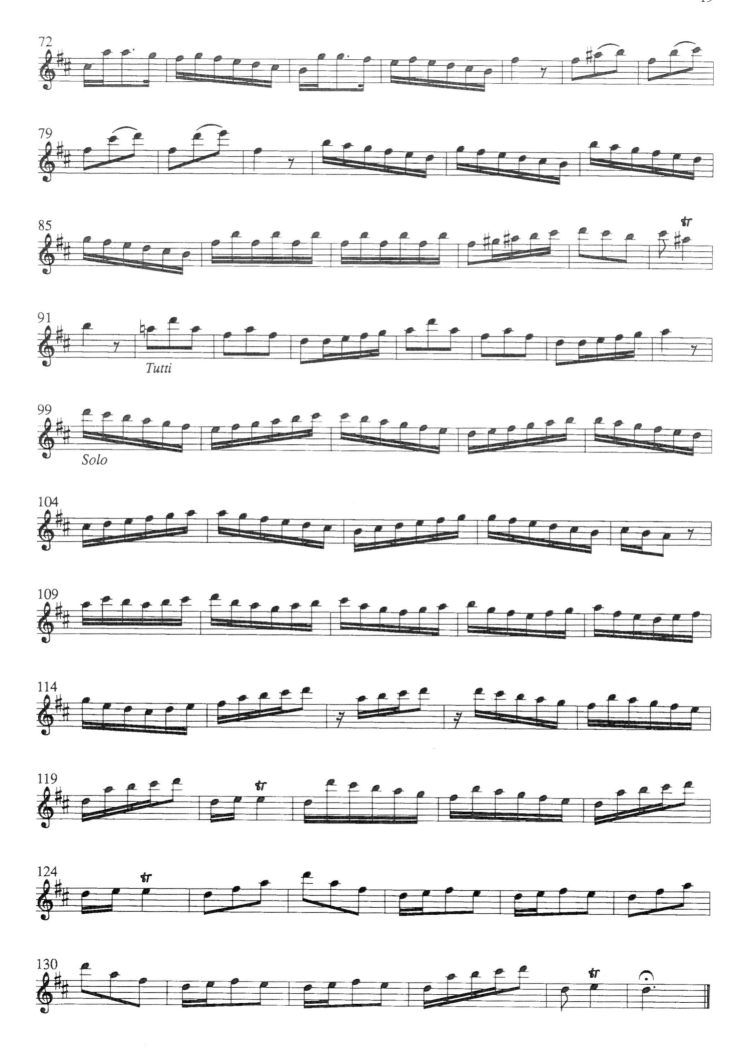

3 FLUTE SONATAS – HANDEL, TELEMANN, MARCELLO

Performed by Rameau Trio: Jean Antrim, flute
Accompaniment: Fortunato Arico, viola da gamba;
Jocelyn Chaparro, harpsichord

These flute sonatas, by three of the great masters of the flute repertoire, will not disappoint. Learn to play wonderful Baroque classics by Händel, Telemann, and Marcello! Includes a printed music score and online audio of two recordings: a complete performance with accompaniment and soloist, and a second version with the accompaniment only...you become the soloist.

00400366 Book/Online Audio $14.99

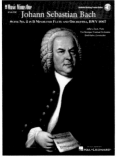

J.S. BACH – SUITE NO. 2 FOR FLUTE & ORCHESTRA B MINOR, BWV1067

Performed by Jeffery Zook, flute
Accompaniment: Stuttgart Festival Orchestra
Conductor: Emil Kahn

Bach's Suite No. 2 is a large-scale Baroque piece in eight movements based on different dance forms. It remains one of the great Baroque works for flute. A must for the repertory of all serious flutists. Includes a printed solo part and access to online audio of the concerto, including demonstration and backing tracks.

00400335 Book/Online Audio............................$14.99

BOSSA, SAMBA AND TANGO DUETS FOR FLUTE & GUITAR

Performed by Katarzyna Bury, flute
Accompaniment: Christian Reichert, guitar;
Jochen Hank, percussion

Here is a collection of Latin masterpieces, arranged for flute, guitar and percussion. From the fabled Granada and François Borne's rousing Fantasy on Themes from Bizet's Carmen, to Brasilian superstar Celso Machado's magnificent Suite Popular Brasileira and Astor Piazzolla's Libertango, there is a wealth of thrilling music for every flutist! Listen to virtuosi Katarzyna Bury and Christian Reichert perform these classic pieces in a complete reference recording. Then you take Ms. Bury's place alongside Mr. Reichert and the percussionist for a Latin music-fest that you will never forget! Bravo!

00400134 Book/Online Audio $19.99

CLASSIC THEMES FROM GREAT COMPOSERS
MUSIC MINUS ONE FLUTE – INTERMEDIATE LEVEL

Accompaniment: Harriet Wingreen, piano

Twenty-seven familiar international world classics for flute and piano. Perfect practice material for the intermediate player. Includes a printed music score and online audio containing the piano accompaniment, minus you, the soloist. Audio is accessed online using the unique code inside the book and can be streamed or downloaded.

00400370 Book/Online Audio $14.99

HÄNDEL – SIX SONATAS FOR FLUTE AND PIANO

Accompaniment: Harriet Wingreen, piano

A collection of Händel's best sonatas for flute (or violin) and piano, brimming with his characteristic classical elegance and charm. Featuring as your accompanist the famed New York Philharmonic pianist Harriet Wingreen, these delightful sonatas are now digitally remastered for unbelievable sonic brilliance! Contains a music score featuring the solo flute (or violin) part and access to online audio containing digitally remastered stereo accompaniments to each sonata.

00400377 Book/Online Audio $14.99

MOZART – FLUTE CONCERTO NO. 2 IN D MAJOR, K. 314; QUANTZ – FLUTE CONCERTO IN G MAJOR

Music Minus One
Performed by Gyorgi Spassov, flute
Accompaniment: Plovdiv Chamber Orchestra
Conductor: Nayden Todorov

MMO presents a brand-new digital recording of one of our all-time best-selling albums: Mozart's magnificent Flute Concerto No. 2 along with Quantz's G-major Concerto. Both are masterpieces at the top of the repertoire. An essential album for every flutist! This deluxe set includes a printed music score and professional recordings of a complete version with soloist; then a second performance of the orchestral accompaniment, minus you, the soloist. The audio is accessed online using the unique code inside each book and can be streamed or downloaded.

00400057 Book/Online Audio $19.99

INTERMEDIATE FLUTE SOLOS – VOLUME 3

Performed by Donald Peck, flute
Accompaniment: Judith Olson, piano

This third volume of intermediate contest solos features the choicest repertoire for flute as performed by Donald Peck of the Chicago Symphony, and then by you, the soloist. Includes Lane's Sonata, Andersen's Scherzino and the Handel Sonata's Allegro movement. Includes a printed music score annotated with performance suggestions and online professional recordings of complete versions (with soloist) followed by piano accompaniment to each piece, minus the soloist.

00400576 Book/Online Audio............................$14.99

PIAZZOLLA: HISTOIRE DU TANGO AND OTHER LATIN CLASSICS FOR FLUTE & GUITAR DUET

Performed by Katarzyna Bury, flute
Accompaniment: Christian Reichert, guitar

Guitar and flute virtuosi Christian Reichert and Katarzyna Bury bring you this album featuring Argentina's most fabled 20th-century tango composer, Astor Piazzolla, who wrote this suite of tango pieces bridging a century of tango styles, drawn in a rich pallette for guitar and flute duet. Alongside this wondrous composition is a quartet of dance classics from such composers as Enrique Granados and Pablo de Sarasate. Sensational music and not to be missed! Includes an authoritative, newly engraved solo part printed on high-quality ivory paper, and online audio recordings featuring a complete version with soloist; then a second version of the orchestral accompaniment, minus the soloist.

00400058 Book/Online Audio $24.99

VIVALDI: THE FOUR SEASONS FOR FLUTE

Performed by Paul Fried, flute
Accompaniment: Czech Symphony Chamber Orchestra
Conductor: Mario Klemens

Here is the classic set of four concerti that sit atop Baroque literature, newly arranged and performed by world-renowned flutist Paul Fried for flute and orchestra. Magnificent in every way, and well worth the effort to learn. Paul performs this perennial classic, then steps aside to permit you to take his place as soloist with the magnificent Czech Symphony Chamber Orchestra under Maestro Mario Klemens. A joy to perform, as well as to listen to, it will delight you for a lifetime! Includes a printed solo part and access to audio tracks online, for download or streaming, using the unique code inside the book

00400672 Book/Online Audio $19.99